Rails to the People's Palace

Reg Davies

The Parkland Walk

David Bevan

Hornsey Historical Society

Hornsey Historical Society,
The Old Schoolhouse,
136 Tottenham Lane,
London N8 7EL

© Hornsey Historical Society 1980, 1985 and 1994

First Published 1980 (printed by the Polytechnic of North London)
Re-printed 1980
Second edition 1985
Third edition 1994

Cover Illustration by Arthur Newstead

ISBN 0 905794 11 7

Printed by J.G. Bryson (Printer) Ltd., 156-164 High Road, London N2 9AS

Introduction

This outline guide covers the railway which used to run from Finsbury Park to Alexandra Palace. It incorporates a history and a trail. It was originally produced as a booklet to go with walks organised by the Hornsey Historical Society and it can be read to accompany any walk along the disused railway.

The author is a North Londoner who attended Stationers' School, now no more. His interest in the line was awakened when as a schoolboy he used to see tube trains travelling along an apparently abandoned railway. With Malcolm Grant, Reg Davies has written two railway books covering this line. *Forgotten railways: Chilterns and Cotswolds* was published by David & Charles in 1975, and revised in 1984, and *London and its railways* appeared in 1983.

By an extraordinary and in one way lucky coincidence the first edition of *Rails to the People's Palace* was published two days after the disastrous fire at Alexandra Palace in July 1980. The public responded immediately and bought the booklet in great numbers. It was re-printed before the end of the year and again sold out. Five years later when the Palace was being re-built, the time was ripe for a second edition.

Stocks of the second edition having been long exhausted a third edition has now been prepared to meet the continuing demand. For this third edition Reg Davies has updated his text. In addition a new section on The Parkland Walk, for which most of the original track is now used, has been added. This section has been commissioned from David Bevan, Conservation Officer for the London Borough of Haringey, who is responsible for the day to day management of the Walk.

And only footsteps in a lane
And birdsong broke the silence round
And chuffs of the Great Northern train
For Alexandra Palace bound

Thoughts on 'The Diary of a Nobody'
John Betjeman

Contents

Illustrations, Maps, Diagrams & Timetables

The Society has also published the following walks:—

Highgate Village – Four Walks by Joan Schwitzer

A Walk Around Muswell Hill by Ken Gay

Hornsey Village – A Walk by Ken Gay

Further Reading:—

Palace on the Hill by Ken Gay
Provides a general history of Alexandra Palace and Park.

Obtainable from Hornsey Historical Society.

Acknowledgements

The Hornsey Historical Society is grateful to the following for permission to reproduce their illustrations:
British Rail (Eastern) for Finsbury Park Station 1950,
Bruce Castle Museum for Last train leaving Alexandra Palace Station 1954,
Michael Cavendish Sleigh, Archivist to the Alexandra Palace Collection, for Alexandra Palace Station c.1900,
David Bevan, for Parkland Walk illustrations, and
Mr. H.C. Casserley for all the remaining photographs.
The HHS would also like to express thanks to Angela Taylor, former Secretary of the Society, who designed the original booklet and arranged its printing, and to Peter Curtis who is responsible for the present edition.

History

After the Great Exhibition of 1851, its building, the 'Crystal Palace', was moved to a permanent site in Sydenham where it soon became a popular place of recreation for those who lived in South London. Inevitably thoughts turned to the provision of something similar in North London, encouraged by the International Exhibition of 1862, whose buildings were used in the erection of an 'Alexandra Palace', named after the Prince of Wales' wife, on the ridge which looks out over Hornsey Vale. The Palace was set in a park, opened in 1863, and its constuction started in 1864, when in anticipation of things to come Wood Green station on the Great Northern Railway (GNR) main line was renamed Wood Green (Alexandra Palace).

In that year too the Edgware, Highgate and London Railway (EH&LR), authorised in 1862 to build a railway from Finsbury Park to Edgware, obtained powers to construct a branch from their line at Highgate to the Alexandra Park boundary in Muswell Hill. Two years later further powers were granted to extend the EH&LR branch from Muswell Hill to the Palace and to link the Palace to the Great Eastern Railway (GER) at Palace Gates station. The link to the GER was to meet the same oblivion as the North London, Highgate & Alexandra Palace Railway, authorised a year earlier in 1865. This was to run from Caledonian Road station on the North London Railway to a connection with the EH&L at Highgate, whose railway it would use to reach Muswell Hill.

Physical and financial difficulties made for slow construction of the Palace and its railway so it was not until 24th May 1873 that both opened. By this time the GNR had taken over the EH&LR and so the double track line from Highgate to Muswell Hill with its continuation to the Palace was operated by the GNR. The EH&L itself was provided with a double track as far as Park Junction from its opening in 1867 and was single from there to Edgware. As the Muswell Hill Estate Company, the owners of the line in the Palace grounds, owned no locomotives or coaches, it had to be operated by the GNR but charged 2d single for the half mile run on its railway.

At first all went well. Huge crowds travelled on the line the day the Palace opened and on Whit Monday, 2 June 1873, 60,000 visited the 1873 Palace, mainly by rail, a greater patronage on that day than Crystal Palace. Alas, sixteen days after it opened, the Palace caught fire and was reduced to rubble. So after 31st July 1873 the train service ceased entirely apart from a daily pick-up goods train running to Muswell Hill if traffic required.

7

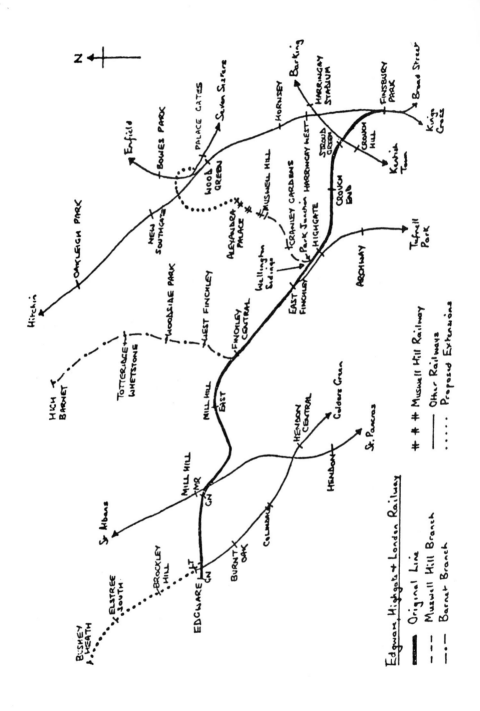

Edgware, Highgate + London Railway

Muswell Hill Railway
———— Other Railways
· · · · · · Proposed Extensions

———— Original Line
– – – Muswell Hill Branch
–·–·– Barnet Branch

N

Hitchin
Oakleigh Park
Enfield
Bowes Park
Palace Gates
Seven Sisters
New Southgate
Wood Green
Hornsey
Harringay West
Harringay Stadium
Barking
Finsbury Park
Broad Street
Kings Cross
Stroud Green
Crouch Hill
Upper Holloway
Alexandra Palace
Muswell Hill
Cranley Gardens
Park Junction
Highgate
Crouch End
Wellington Sidings
Tufnell Park
Woodside Park
West Finchley
Finchley Central
East Finchley
Archway
Totteridge + Whetstone
High Barnet
Mill Hill East
Mill Hill (LMR)
Mill Hill GN
St Albans
Hendon Central
Golders Green
Hendon
St Pancras
Burnt Oak
Colindale
Edgware (GN)
Edgware (LT)
Brockley Hill
Elstree South
Bushey Heath

8

Rebuilding of the Palace began in 1874 and for its opening on 1st May 1875 train services were restored, including a service from Broad Street provided by the North London Railway. 21,000 people visited the Palace on opening day but most of the following Whit Monday's 94,000 visitors had cause to regret they came by rail. The journey from Kings's Cross took an hour and a derailment in the evening caused some to walk off the railway and others to sleep on the trains.

Whilst modest success attended the Palace and its railway in the 1870s, the next decade saw a decline as the public grew tired of its attractions and only thronged there on Bank Holidays. To try and revive its fortunes, the London Financial Association, the owner of the Palace, attempted to sell off part of the Park for housing, with little success. As access to the terminus was restricted to patrons of the Palace, the shareholders in the railway were incorporated into a separate undertaking, the Muswell Hill & Palace Railway, in 1886. This enabled the terminus to be operated as a public railway station to aid any housing development.

But the Palace continued its decline. It closed for considerable periods in the 1880s and from 1889 to 1898. During this time the branch services terminated at Muswell Hill, but in the hope of suburban development the GNR opened the terminus once more in March 1891. Business was poor and it closed in April 1892. Finally in 1898 the GNR agreed that the Palace station should re-open continuously and the railway helped to carry the 100,000 that came that Easter Monday to see the Palace, newly emerged from its slumbers.

Weary of their burden the Palace owners offered their undertaking to a consortium of local authorities, which would appoint Trustees. The transactions were completed in February 1901 when 173 acres passed to the Trustees and the rest was sold for building. Modest prosperity returned under the new regime and the GNR purchased the Muswell Hill & Palace Railway in 1911.

By the turn of the century, London had grown northwards and stood on the brink of Muswell Hill. To provide for earlier growth the GNR had provided a new station at Stroud Green in 1881, and on 2nd August 1902 Cranley Gardens was opened. Building activity was considerable in the first two decades of the twentieth century in Muswell Hill. Building materials, coal, and goods for the shops provided the branch with valuable freight traffic. Indeed, light railways were laid so that main line wagons filled with materials could be hauled by contractors' locomotives to deposit the materials at each plot.

Alexandra Palace Station, June 1937.

The influence of the railway could be seen in the population figures. Hornsey grew from 19,380 in 1871 to 44,523 in 1891 whilst the growth at Muswell Hill was even more dramatic. There were 1,500 people in the area when the railway arrived in 1873; this figure climbed gradually to 5,833 in 1901 and virtually doubled to 11,335 in the next ten years. With growth came administrative change. Hornsey became an Urban District Council in 1894 and a borough in 1903. By 1911, 84,592 people were contained within its boundaries.

However, topography had dictated the roundabout nature of the line and more direct forms of transport began to make an appearance. Tramways were first, opening from Turnpike Lane to the bottom of Muswell Hill in 1905 and from Wood Green to the east entrance of the Palace in 1906. London General Omnibus Co. ("General") bus services from Muswell Hill to the tube stations at Finsbury Park and Archway (opened in 1904 and 1907 respectively) abstracted considerable traffic from the branch. Despite the GNR obtaining an injunction to keep down the weight, and therefore the size, of the General buses going over the road bridges at Crouch End and Cranley Gardens, the competition grew as the General merely ran more. As the buses offered through bookings to the Underground, their attraction grew in the 'twenties.

10

Some measure of the effects of competition can be seen from a GNR survey of ordinary bookings from the branch stations.

	March 1914	March 1919	Change
Stroud Green	26,005	31,453	+5,448
Crouch End	62,349	38,820	-23,529
Highgate	19,843	10,277	-9,566
Cranley Gardens	12,948	5,995	-6,953
Muswell Hill	20,051	7,017	-13,034
Alexandra Palace	4,392	2,622	-2,130

The considerable reductions at Crouch End and Muswell Hill are immediately apparent. Significantly March 1914 was the last full month before the introduction of General route 111, a precursor of today's W7. As this ran from Muswell Hill through Crouch End to Finsbury Park it must have abstracted considerable traffic from the branch.

The Palace had an eventful War. It became successively a holding centre for army reservists, a refugee camp and an internment camp. Immediately after the War it was used by the Civil Service. In 1915 its weekday railway service was reduced to principally a shuttle from Finsbury Park but in 1919 GNR services were restored in full. Sunday services which had been suspended in 1915 had to wait until 1925 for restoration, although by 1930 they had been withdrawn in the face of bus competition.

Alexandra Park re-opened in 1920 and the Palace two years later. However, it was the same old story. The popularity of the Palace continued to decline and the Trustees were unable to keep it in repair. The London and North Eastern Railway (LNER), which had absorbed the GNR in 1923, was blamed for providing poor transport facilities. In 1930 Sundays often saw 6,000 visitors to the Park, yet the LNER provided no trains, and of 30,000 visitors one Bank Holiday, only 150 had arrived by train.

Even commuter traffic declined. The number of annual season tickets sold at Stroud Green fell from 947 in 1925 to 690 in 1929 and at Crouch End from 1,736 to 1,304 in the same period. Yet there were the beginnings of social change in Hornsey by 1930, as some of the larger houses were split into flats as domestic help became in short supply. The 1931 population was 95,416 and nearly a quarter of the working population were clerks. The potential market was there but the message was clear. The population had deserted the branch for the bus and the tube.

June 1935 brought the promise of a brighter future. As part of a government programme of works to relieve unemployment Neville Chamberlain, the Chancellor of the Exchequer, announced that the

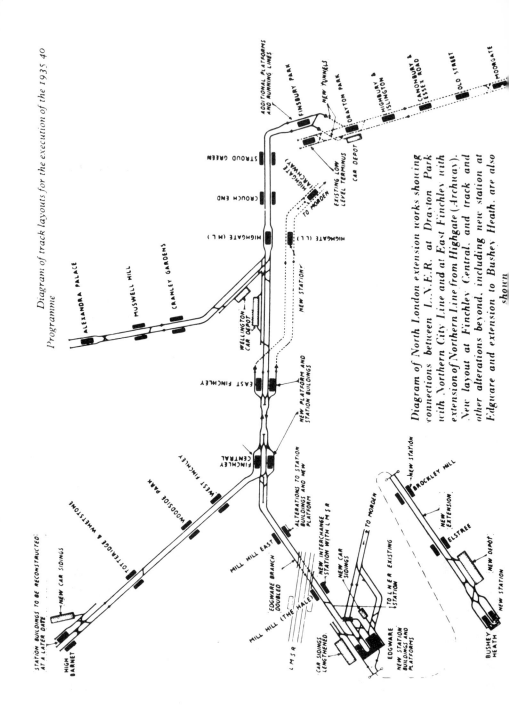

Diagram of track layouts for the execution of the 1935-40 Programme

ALEXANDRA PALACE

MUSWELL HILL

CRANLEY GARDENS

STROUD GREEN

CROUCH END

HIGHGATE (H.L.)

HIGHGATE (L.L.)

WELLINGTON CAR DEPOT

EAST FINCHLEY

NEW PLATFORM AND STATION BUILDINGS

FINCHLEY CENTRAL

WEST FINCHLEY

WOODSIDE PARK

ALTERATIONS TO STATION BUILDINGS AND NEW PLATFORM

TOTTERIDGE & WHETSTONE

STATION BUILDINGS TO BE RECONSTRUCTED AT A LATER DATE

NEW CAR SIDINGS

HIGH BARNET

MILL HILL EAST

EDGWARE BRANCH DOUBLED

MILL HILL (THE HALE)

L M S R

NEW INTERCHANGE STATION WITH L M S R

NEW CAR SIDINGS

TO MORDEN

CAR SIDINGS LENGTHENED

TO LNER EXISTING STATION

EDGWARE
NEW STATION BUILDINGS AND PLATFORMS

NEW STATION

NEW STATION

NEW EXTENSION

ELSTREE

NEW DEPOT

NEW STATION

BROCKLEY HILL

BUSHEY HEATH

ADDITIONAL PLATFORMS AND RUNNING LINES

FINSBURY PARK

NEW TUNNELS

DRAYTON PARK

CAR DEPOT

EXISTING LOW LEVEL TERMINUS

HIGHGATE (ARCHWAY)

TO MORDEN

NEW STATION

HIGHBURY & ISLINGTON

CANONBURY & ESSEX ROAD

OLD STREET

MOORGATE

Diagram of North London extension works showing connections between L.N.E.R. at Drayton Park with Northern City Line and at East Finchley with extension of Northern Line from Highgate (Archway). New layout at Finchley Central, and track and other alterations beyond, including new station at Edgware and extension to Bushey Heath, are also shown

branch was to be electrified as a part of the Northern line of the Underground system. There would be six trains an hour (seven in the rush hour) from Alexandra Palace to Finsbury Park and onward to Moorgate via a new connection to the former Great Northern & City Railway (GN&CR). The tube was to be extended from Archway to join the LNER line at East Finchley with a new station at Highgate under the LNER surface station, which would itself be reconstructed. Northern line passengers were expected to increase from 150 to 180 million a year when the whole scheme was complete.

Work on the scheme was well advanced at the outbreak of war in September 1939. Some indications of the progress made is shown by the press preview held on 28 June 1939 where Lord Ashfield, Chairman of the London Passenger Transport Board (LPTB), and Sir Ronald Matthews, Chairman of the LNER, acted as hosts. Sir Ronald drove a 'special' from Archway to East Finchley and the party inspected the incomplete Highgate station. Lunch was taken at the *White Lion*, which had been re-sited to enable the railway bridge at East Finchley to be widened.

Alexandra Palace Station c.1900 before reconstruction by the GNR

13

At first wartime conditions merely slowed progress. In November 1939 a LPTB review of the partly-completed parts of the New Works Programme decided to postpone electrification from Finsbury Park to Alexandra Palace, but in 1940 all work was suspended 'for the duration'. Initially Alexandra Palace services were cut but when the tube was extended to High Barnet in April 1940, LNER steam trains normally ran to the Palace and only reached East Finchley in the rush hour. After Highgate tube station opened in 1941 (having opened in 1940 as an air raid shelter) all LNER services ran to Alexandra Palace as East Finchley and stations beyond could be reached by changing onto the tube at Highgate. However, cuts in the service in 1942 left only a weekday rush hour service from Finsbury Park to Alexandra Palace.

Peace returned to find little unfinished work. At Finsbury Park the new connection to the former GN&CR, two road overbridges and the new tube platforms awaited completion. Indeed the Seven Sisters Road bridge had been delivered to the site ready for erection. Conductor rails and lineside cabling had been laid for much of the way. Sub-station buildings at Crouch End and Muswell Hill awaited equipping, as did the new signalbox at Park Junction, while the new subsidiary signalboxes at Alexandra Palace and Cranley Gardens were well begun. Station work had started at Stroud Green, Church End and Highgate (surface station), where the tracks had been raised so tube trains could operate.

Work seemed slow to resume and a Parliamentary reply gave the need to restrict capital investment as the reason. An LPTB Committee, set up to review progress with the 1935 Plan, recommended in 1947 that electrification to Alexandra Palace should be completed, an intention confirmed two years later by a Working Party looking at all London's rail facilities. However, temporary closure of the Palace line in the winter of 1951-52 was an ill omen. Although restored in January 1952, the service was liable to delay and cancellation. So it came as no surprise when London Transport (LT) announced in Autumn 1953 that the proposals for the Alexandra Palace line were cancelled. Buses were capable of providing a quicker, more frequent and more attractive service than the branch. The local authorities and the Palace Trustees were told that the 700 passengers who used the line from Mondays to Fridays could not justify its retention and a further £2m would be needed to finish the pre-war plans. Somehow the threefold increase in traffic on the Barnet line after electrification was forgotten and, despite protests, the last passenger train ran on 3rd July 1954. In 1954 too LT announced the formal abandonment of all the unfinished parts of the 1935 Plan.

Some conductor rail had been removed in 1952 for use on the Upminster line, stated to be because of the difficulty of obtaining new rails, and the rest was removed by 1955. Goods traffic and enthusiasts' specials kept the line alive for a time but Muswell Hill goods yard closed in 1956 and Cranley

14

Gardens a year later. Goods services continued to use the section from Finsbury Park to Park Junction and on to East Finchley until withdrawn from Edgware and Barnet in 1964. Thereafter it was used solely to transfer London Transport Northern line tube cars from Wellington Sidings depot to the former GN&CR at Drayton Park, left isolated by the non-completion of the 1935 Plan. Eventually the poor condition of the bridge meant these workings had to be diverted to another route, the last running on 29th September 1970. By the end of 1971 the rails between Finsbury Park and Highgate were removed and the tunnel mouth at Highgate sealed, leaving Wellington Sidings at the end of a stub from East Finchley.

Route

Throughout this description, reference will be made to the up and down directions. Trains from Alexandra Palace to Finsbury Park used the up line whilst those in the reverse direction used the down. Similarly, passengers would catch a train going towards Finsbury Park from the up platform, or if they wanted to go to the Palace from the down platform.

The branch started on either side of the GNR main line at Finsbury Park. Trains from London climbed on arches constucted between two slow lines to join the track to London, immediately before the latter crossed the main lines by a bridge and then descended alongside the Park to the extreme east side of the station. The 1935 Plan would have altered this arrangement so that both tracks would have crossed the main line and run into a new platform to the east of the existing platform before going on to new ramp connections to the GN&CR at Drayton Park (at 1 in 45 northbound and 1 in 50 southbound). It was intended to build a new booking hall at Finsbury Park underneath the girder work that supported the new platform and to present an imposing facade to Station Road. To-day all traces of the girder work, the only part actually to be erected, have disappeared and a bus station has been built on the site.

Leaving Finsbury Park No.7 signal box where the two tracks joined, the line crossed Tollington Park on an overbridge and ran on an embankment to Stroud Green station which, like all the intermediate stations, except Highgate, had two side platforms. Here the booking office was built on the north side of Stapleton Hall Road and a flight of steps ascended to the wooden buildings. As the station dealt with passenger traffic only, no goods facilities were provided. Travelling onwards, the line passed from embankment to cutting and began to climb at 1 in 72. Gradients were against the locomotive all the way from Finsbury Park to Highgate and trains were time-tabled to take two minutes longer when travelling in this direction.

Highgate's New Station

UNDERGROUND UNDER L·N·E·R
ESCALATOR TO ALEXANDRA PALACE LINE

After crossing Mount Pleasant Villas, embankment gave way to cutting as the line passed under Mount View Road and Crouch Hill to run into Crouch End station where a number of footpaths radiated from the station to the large houses of this desirable late-Victorian suburb. A small amount of building had commenced on the wooded slopes near the railway when the Edgware line opened in 1867 and at Christ Church, erected in 1862, the church wardens were pressing ahead with an extension. The station was in a shallow cutting and the brick booking office led to a footbridge down to the two platforms. Reconstruction as part of the 1935 Plans lowered the platforms to tube train door height.

Trains for the Palace resumed their climb after a stop at Crouch End, tackling a maximum gradient of 1 in 59. Cutting was replaced by embankment as the line crossed Stanhope Road but was resumed as Highgate was approached. On either side of Highgate station were two sets of single-bore tunnels and the station itself nestled under Archway Road. As it was originally intended as an intermediate terminus, the two platforms were built sufficiently far apart for a siding track between the platform lines. Increasing traffic lead to a rebuilding around 1880 when the side platforms were replaced by a central island. Access to it was gained from a booking office on the footbridge which led to entrances on both sides of the line.

A further rebuilding came as part of the 1935 Plans under which Highgate was to become a two-level station dealing with 35 trains in the peak hour. 21 of these would be dealt with at the two deep-level platforms on the tube extension from Archway to East Finchley and 14 at the existing surface-level station. A contract was let in March 1940 for the reconstruction of the surface-level buildings in the typical LPTB style, and from this island platform a staircase led down to a circulating area directly beneath the tracks. Access from Priory Gardens and Archway Road was provided to this circulating area which contained the booking office and from which escalators ran to the deep-level platforms sixty feet below. 490 feet long, these platforms were capable of accommodating nine-car trains.

Steps led down the sixty feet from Archway Road to the circulating area, supplemented by a path from Wood Lane to Priory Gardens. Passengers, promised an escalator from the circulating area up to Archway Road as part of the original plans, had to wait until 1957 before they obtained it. Even then the exit by The Woodman was not surmounted by the statue of Dick Whittington originally envisaged. Most of the station is still unchanged, although the surface platform became disused with the withdrawal of the Alexandra Palace service and access to it from the circulating area was subsequently eliminated.

Highgate Station, June 1937

Almost immediately to the north of the second tunnel, the Alexandra Palace line parted company with the Barnet and Edgware line at Park Junction. To the west of the former line, adjacent to Archway Road, was Highgate Goods Yard whilst in the fork between the two lines was Wellington Sidings. The LNER kept the Royal Train here but when the depot was taken over by the tube, the LPTB had to pay for replacement buildings for the LNER alongside the main line at Wood Green. Further stabling for tube trains was provided in the sidings laid parallel to the Alexandra Palace branch.

Leaving the junction the Palace branch curved east along the edge of Highgate Wood and entered Cranley Gardens station. Its wooden booking office was on the west side of Muswell Hill Road and a footbridge led to the platforms with their wood and brick buildings. A separate pedestrian exit was also provided from the down platform to the corner of Muswell Hill Road and Woodside Avenue. Here again, footpaths led to the station. Behind the down platform was the goods yard hidden by a line of trees. Nowadays housing occupies the station site whilst a school has been built in the former goods yard.

Under the road bridge the tracks gradually emerged from the cutting on to a 17-arch brick viaduct, crossing St. James's Lane, and looking towards the ridge the line had pierced at Highgate. Immediately after passing under the Hill the line entered Muswell Hill station. Very conveniently situated for the shopping centre it had a small forecourt off the bridge. The brick booking office had stairs leading to each platform but rush-hour travellers could use another entrance from Dukes Avenue. The small goods yard behind the up platform required goods trains coming from Highgate to reverse to gain access. Today a primary school uses both the station and the entrance from Dukes Avenue.

Onwards the branch ran mainly in a shallow cutting as the Palace loomed up on the right. Passing the signal box on the left, immediately before the bridge over one of the Park roads, the line ran into its terminus. Originally the platforms were beneath a terrace alongside the north-west front and this survived the 1873 fire. By the 1900s the interior with its wooden platforms had become so dilapidated the GNR had to rebuild it. The terrace was demolished except for a flight of entrance steps leading into The Avenue beside the station building. The island platform was rebuilt in shortened form and given an awning, whilst the third platform became a carriage siding. The two-track goods yard along the north sides of the station was principally used for coal to heat the Palace. To provide electricity for the tube extensions, a 11 kv 50 c/s supply was provided from the North Metropolitan Electric Supply Co. at Wood Green to the main sub-station at East Finchley. The three high-tension cables were laid the Palace grounds and along the branch to Park Junction to reach LT. After closure, a British Rail technical laboratory was built on part of the Palace station site whilst car auctions took place on the remainder. Only the station building remains, which together with the now demolished signal box was the only structure of architectural note.

Train Services

Beacause the section between Finsbury Park and Highgate was common to the Alexandra Palace, Edgware and Barnet services, this section is divided into two parts: services to the Palace and services to Edgware and Barnet.

The Alexandra Palace Limited at Finsbury Park Station, July 1950

Alexandra Palace

On the opening of the branch the GNR provided a service of eighteen trains a day each way. Sightseers to the Palace ruins were provided for a short period with the reduced service of seven trains each way but soon all trains were withdrawn, leaving only a goods train to run as far as Muswell Hill if traffic required. Since the residents of the area at that time were few and well-to-do, they could go by carriage to Highgate or Wood Green stations.

When the Palace re-opened in 1875 GNR trains were fully restored together with a North London Railway (NLR) service from Broad Street. This reached the GNR at Finsbury Park by means of a spur, opened in 1874, which left the NLR at Canonbury. The vicissitudes to which the Palace was subjected in the 1880s had their effect on its railway. Whenever the Palace was closed, services terminated at Muswell Hill.

By 1910 there were sixty-one trains each way daily on the branch. Not all ran right the way through to the Palace terminus, whilst twenty of them were NLR Broad Street trains. GNR services ran either to King's Cross or Moorgate via Farringdon. The first departure from Muswell Hill was at 7.14 am. and the last arrival 12.16 am., the former clearly pointing out the middle class nature of the district. Working class areas had the first train much earlier in the mornings.

Because of the heavy demand of wartime freight traffic, off-peak trains to Moorgate and King's Cross were cancelled and from 1915 the service was reduced to a shuttle between Alexandra Palace and Finsbury Park outside the morning and evening peaks. NLR off-peak trains also ceased, only making a brief appearance after the war before final withdrawal. After 1919, GNR services were fully restored continuing little changed until the outbreak of World War II. By 1939 there were around forty trains daily each way including London Midland & Scottish Railway (LMSR) peak hour services to Broad Street, as the NLR had been merged into the LMSR in 1923. Sunday trains had been suspended in 1915 but reappeared from 1925 to 1930.

Apart from the GNR's experimental use of American-built tender locomotives for a short period at the turn of the century, trains were almost exclusively hauled by tank locomotives. The GNR (later LNER) services came to be hauled in the 1920s by the N2 Class 0-6-2- tanks designed by Sir Nigel Gresley and these provided the mainstay of the service until its withdrawal. NLR services were normally headed by William Adams' 4-4-0 tanks, a design unique to that railway. They were replaced in LMSR days by 0-6-0 tanks to the design of Sir Henry Fowler. Four-wheel coaches lasted on the NLR services well after the end of World War I, whilst the LNER provided sets of articulated coaches, designed to make passengers sit bolt upright.

As part of the Underground system, the line was expected to be served by eight-car trains of new tube rolling stock. Orders were placed for 750 cars of this '1938 stock', so called as the first train was delivered to Golders Green tube depot in May 1938. The first train went into regular service on 30th June 1938. Additional orders brought the total order to 1121 cars of which the LNER owned 289. This was regarded as the company's share for operating the Edgware, Barnet and Alexandra Palace services and their ownership was indicated by a plate on the sole-bar of their cars. These trains, whilst they did not operate to Alexandra Palace or to Edgware via Mill Hill, continued to operate Northern line train services until finally replaced in 1978.

Stroud Green Station, August 1945

With the outbreak of war, the branch Monday to Friday services were cut by over a half, and through trains to Moorgate and Broad Street ceased from 10th September 1939 in the expectation of a wartime fall in commuting. The latter returned on 4th December but ceased permanently on 3rd October 1940 as a result of severe bomb damage to the North London lines. When the tube reached High Barnet in April 1940, the LNER service ran only to East Finchley in the rush hour and the remainder of the service ran to Alexandra Palace. From March 1941 all LNER services ran to Alexandra Palace but from September 1942, all through trains were withdrawn, leaving only three an hour shuttling to and from Finsbury Park in the weekday peaks. Trains did not run after 7.00 pm., and on Saturdays services ceased at 5.00 pm.

The return of peace enabled a slightly better service to be provided but even in 1950 there was a four-hour gap in the service at mid-day and last trains still obeyed their wartime curfew. All services were withdrawn between October 1951 and January 1952. On resumption of service there were fifteen down trains and seventeen up, a few starting or finishing at Highgate, and the gap in the service remained. Services were exiguous with tank engines pushing or pulling two gas-lit coaches. Despite through bookings from all tube stations, introduced in anticipation of the tube conversion, the limited nature of the service discouraged traffic. Printed tickets to tube stations on the High Barnet line were issued at Finsbury Park for travel via Highgate in the early 1950s but the facility was little known or used. Introduction in 1952 of fares based on mileage travelled hardly favoured the line. Because of its circuitous route, fares to Alexandra Palace from King's Cross or Broad Street were 50% above those to Wood Green station on the main line.

The last pasenger train ran on 3rd July 1954 when eight gas-lit coaches were hauled by a N2 tank locomotive. Jerky starts from Stroud Green and Crouch End caused a drawbar fracture when the train attempted to leave Highgate, so another N2 had to be commandeered from a following freight to propel the train to Alexandra Palace. The original locomotive was restored for the return trip which arrived at Finsbury Park, fittingly 35 minutes late. Goods trains and specials were to run a little longer but all activity had finished by 1957.

From *Bradshaw's Railway Guide* August 1887

Eastern Region	FINSBURY PARK—ALEXANDRA PALACE Third class only.	70

WEEKDAYS—MORNING.

WEEKDAYS—AFTERNOON

WEEKDAYS—MORNING

WEEKDAYS—AFTERNOON

NO SUNDAY TRAINS

* Passengers can arrive at 8.15 a.m., change at Welwyn Garden City. § Passengers can depart Hatfield 7.13 p.m. (7.22 on Friday), change at Welwyn Garden City. ‡ Change at Welwyn Garden City ; arrives 4.53 p.m. on Monday, Friday and Saturday. A Arrives 6 minutes earlier. B Arrives 4 minutes earlier. C Arrives 3 minutes earlier. D Arrives 7 minutes earlier. FO Friday only. FSX Not Friday or Saturday. FX Not Friday. H Arrives 5 minutes earlier. J 6 minutes earlier on Friday. SO Saturday only. SX or E Not Saturday. T Through train to Finsbury Park and Broad Street.

ALL TRAINS SHOWN ABOVE HAVE 3rd CLASS ACCOMMODATION ONLY, UNLESS OTHERWISE MARKED.

From *The ABC Railway Guide*, February 1949

155

24

Edgware and Barnet

When the EH&L opened in August 1867 there were eighteen trains daily each way between Finsbury Park and Highgate, of which eight reversed at Highgate and ten ran through to Edgware. Some ran to King's Cross, whilst others terminated at Finsbury Park. When the double line was extended to East Finchley in December 1867 Highgate ceased to be an intermediate terminus. Trains were extended to Farringdon and Ludgate Hill in February 1868 and on the opening of the Barnet line in 1872 there were twenty-four trains a day each way, all but one terminating at High Barnet. The exception travelled to Edgware, whose service was otherwise reduced to a shuttle from Finchley Central. Throughout the 1870s a gradual increase in train services, caused by surburban growth, strained the line capacity between Finsbury Park and King's Cross. This was partially eased when NLR trains to and from Broad Street appeared on the Barnet branch from 1875.

By 1911 Finchley Central had 60 trains daily each way but tram and bus competition were beginning to erode traffic on the Barnet line in conjuction with tube at Golders Green. Building in the 1920s and 1930s put more pressure on rush hour services but about the only improvement was the introduction of colour light signalling between Finsbury Park and Park Junction in 1932. This assisted trains running in fog and enabled the signal boxes at Stroud Green, Crouch End, Archway and Highgate to be closed. By 1938 there were some fifty - five trains a day each way on the High Barnet branch which in some cases ran non-stop through the stations from Highgate to Finsbury Park.

Freight traffic remained important in the 1930s although materials to construct the houses and roads of the new suburbs began to decline by the end of the decade. In 1938 there were about ten goods trains daily to the Edgware and Barnet branches, usually hauled by tender locomotives. A special traffic was milk brought nightly from Staffordshire to the United Dairies depot at East Finchley. Starting in 1928 it lasted for twenty years before being replaced by road transport.

Introduction of the tube service to High Barnet eliminated LNER services beyond East Finchley and, after the opening of Highgate deep level station in 1941, they were all diverted to Alexandra Palace. After closure of the Palace branch, all that remained between Finsbury Park and Highgate were goods and special trains to Edgware and Barnet.

Cranley Gardens Station, June 1937

Operating goods trains, by now hauled by N2 tank locomotives, in between a busy tube service presented certain problems. They were limited to 40 m.p.h. between Finsbury Park and Park Junction where they had exclusive use of the tracks. However, signalling on the LT lines was based on braking distances of tube trains which were shorter than goods trains. In order to overcome this, freights were limited to 20 m.p.h. over LT tracks, and distant signals were erected to give advance warning of the aspect of the next signal. All BR locomotives had to be fitted with tripcock apparatus which was capable of applying the brakes if the train passed a signal at danger. To test this apparatus, equipment was provided on the down platform at Highgate surface level station. It took the form of a white light beneath the starting signal which would be extinguished if the tripcock were detected in the correct position. If the light remained illuminated after the locomotive had passed over the treadle of the testing apparatus, the tripcock had to be examined as soon as possible.

Specials were limited to seaside excusions or railway enthusiast trips and these generally brought tender engines to the line. As the LT Northern City line was left isolated, all tube cars destined for major maintenance had to be moved over BR lines. They were first hauled up the ramp from Drayton Park and made up into a goods train at Highbury Vale Yard. Often they would travel out to Edgware and return to LT hands at Wellington Sidings on the return trip. Diesel locomotives began to be used on these goods trains from late 1960 and by March 1961 scheduled use of steam locomotives had ceased. The withdrawal of goods services from Edgware in 1964 left these tube workings as the sole users of the line from Finsbury Park to Highgate. In 1971 these were diverted via King's Cross, the route they took until the end of LT services on the Northern City line in 1975, to enable closure of the section from Finsbury Park to Highgate.

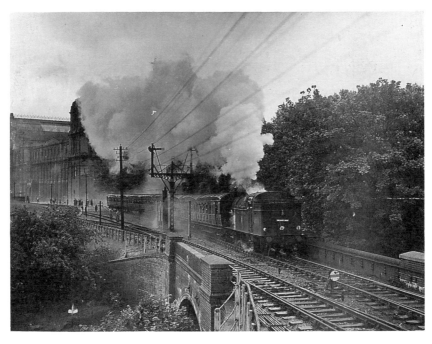

Last train leaving Alexandra Palace Station 1954

Gazetteer

Miles	Station	Opened to Passengers	Closed to Passengers	Closed to Goods	See Note No.
—	Seven Sisters Road	1 Jul 1861	—	1 Apr 1968	1 and 2
$\frac{3}{4}$	Stroud Green	11 Apr 1881	5 Jul 1954	—	3
$1\frac{1}{4}$	Crouch End	22 Aug 1867	5 Jul 1954	—	3
$2\frac{1}{4}$	Highgate	22 Aug 1867	5 Jul 1954	1 Oct 1962	3 and 4
3	Cranley Gardens	2 Aug 1902	5 Jul 1954	18 May 1957	3
$3\frac{3}{4}$	Muswell Hill	24 May 1873	5 Jul 1954	14 Jun 1956	5
$4\frac{1}{4}$	Alexandra Palace	24 May 1873	5 Jul 1954	—	6

Notes

1. Renamed Finsbury Park 1st January 1870.
2. Private siding remained open after closure to public goods traffic.
3. Closed to passengers from 29th October 1951 and re-opened on 7th January 1952.
4. Goods depot re-named Highgate Wellington Sidings 1954.
5. Closed to passengers from July 1873 and re-opened on 1st May 1875; closed again from 29th October 1951 and re-opened on 7th January 1952.

6.

Closed to Passengers from	Re-opened to Passengers on	
Jul. 1873	1 May 1875	
Nov. 1876	10 May 1877	
Aug. 1882	Apr. 1885	
Sep. 1885	Jun. 1887	
Sep. 1887	12 May 1888	
Nov. 1888	Jun. 1889	
Aug. 1889	Mar. 1891	(re-opened as Alexandra Park)
Apr. 1892	1 Apr. 1898	(re-opened as Alexandra Palace)
29 Oct. 1951	7 Jan. 1952	

Bibliography

Bruce, J. Graeme *The Big Tube* (1976).

Carrington, R. *Alexandra Park and Palace – A history* (1975)

Davies, R. and Grant, M.D. *Forgotten Railways: Chilterns and Cotswolds*
(Newton Abbot, 1975, revised edition 1984).

London and its Railways (Newton Abbot, 1983).

Jackson, Alan A. *London's Local Railways* (Newton Abbot, 1978).

Jackson, Alan A. and Croome, Desmond F. *Rails through the clay*

Wilmot, George *The Railway in Finchley: a study in suburban development*
(Hendon, 1973).

Young, John N. *Great Northern Suburban* (Newton Abbot, 1977).

The Parkland Walk

The Longest Nature Reserve in the Capital

Much of the former railway land lying between Finsbury Park and Alexandra Palace has now been developed as a unique green walkway known as the Parkland Walk. The land was acquired by Haringey Council in three stages. The first, between Highgate Wood and Alexandra Palace (including the massive St. James's Lane viaduct with its fine views) was quickly adopted as the beginning of the Walk. The second stage, from Archway Road to Finsbury Park was achieved with greater difficulty. It was originally intended to create a footpath, natural open space and housing, but the latter aroused widespread opposition leading to a public inquiry in 1978. The outcome of the inquiry was a decision against the housing, but in favour of maintaining "the natural character of the area" as a valuable amenity. In 1980 the Council appointed David Hope as warden. A third section was purchased from British Rail in 1986 which allowed the Walk to be extended southwards from the Oxford Road footbridge to a new entrance on Stroud Green Road. This was officially opened in October 1989, completing an unbroken two and a half mile stretch of walk between Finsbury Park Station and Holmesdale Road in Highgate (see Map).

Crouch End Station Platform looking East

In 1980 the newly appointed warden faced an enormous challenge. Much of the land had become derelict since the rails were taken up in 1971.

Widespread dumping of rubbish had occurred and in many places the old track was flooded where land drains had become blocked. The trackway itself was in poor condition and required extensive re-surfacing work. By 1984, assisted by a team of three full-time parks staff, the warden (newly promoted as London's first borough Conservation Officer), had achieved a remakable transformation. The re-surfacing work had been completed and new access pathways and steps were constructed. An Information Centre had been set up in the original Station House at Stroud Green and the Parkland Walk itself was officially opened.

From the start, management work has been directed at maintaining and enhancing the diversity of natural habitats that have developed since the closure of the railway. The grassy embankments and cuttings which characterised the working railway had been maintained by regular cutting and burning. When this ceased following the closure of the railway, tall herbs, brambles, and other shrubs were able to colonise and the nature of the vegetation slowly changed. This was welcome because it provided different habitats for a new range of plants and animals. Nevertheless, if this process had been allowed to continue unchecked, the Parkland Walk would eventually have become dominated throughout by dense woodland and the current variety of habitat would be lost. Management therefore seeks to hold this natural succession of vegetation at different stages, so that the Walk presents a mosaic of different habitats varying from the original open grassland, through taller herbaceous plants to scrub and woodland. Each area supports its own array of wildlife.

The development of the Parkland Walk has not been without incident. In the mid 1980s it came under increasing threat from the Department of Transport's East London Assessment Study which proposed the construction of a 6-lane motorway along the Walk. This met with fierce opposition from the Council and local people. A campaign to "save the Walk" was spear-headed by the newly founded Friends of the Parkland Walk. By December 1989 the Department of Transport had backed off, agreeing that the proposals would have "unacceptable environmental consequences". Nevertheless, their modified proposals included plans for a "bored tunnel". Such an undertaking would have been enormously costly and was never a realistic option. It was widely regarded as something of a "face saver" and the proposals were quietly dropped in 1990.

In November of that year, the Council declared the Walk a Local Nature Reserve under the provisions of the National Parks and Access to the Countryside Act of 1949. This statutory designation confers considerable protection to the Walk.

Crouch End Station looking NW to Crouch End Hill

The Parkland Walk has won a number of awards in recent years including the prestigious Inner City Improvement Trophy, presented by the London Tourist Board in 1990. One of the judges commented that "the Walk is just the sort of rural development that is desperately needed in urban areas, where wild flowers can grow, with trees and squirrels on hand so that one does not have to travel far into the countryside to enjoy them. The vision of the Parkland Walk inspired all the judges".

In April 1991 the Parkland Walk faced a more insidious threat when the Conservation Unit, responsible for its management, became one casualty of the widespread Council cutbacks. The unit was disbanded and the Information Centre closed. Since that time the high standard of upkeep along the Walk inevitably declined. As a consequence, many of the formerly open grassy embankments have been invaded by scrub and the previous diversity of habitats has tended to slowly decline.

However the Council re-appointed the Conservation Officer in April 1992, albeit with slender resources and no staff. Nevertheless, with the enthusiastic voluntary support of the Friends of the Parkland Walk and the regular help of the British Trust for Conservation Volunteers, the process of decline has been halted.

There is a considerable diversity of fauna and flora on the Walk (see Bantock, C.R. [ed], *The Ecology of Open Spaces in Haringey,* The Polytechnic of North London, 1984). More than three hundred different kinds of wild flower have now been recorded. They range from the commonplace to the exotic. Orchids rub shoulders with Dandelions and Ivy clambers up Fig trees. Many of the introduced plants have escaped from local gardens. They include the Michaelmas Daisies and Golden Rods from North America, which colour the embankments with blue and yellow in late summer. Perhaps the most striking is the Buddleia. This originates from Western China, where it is found growing on the sides of cliffs. Introduced in the late 19th century as an ornamental garden shrub, its light, wind-dispersed seeds quickly enabled it to establish colonies on the artificial cliff sides of old buildings, railway brickwork and the like. It is a notable feature of such places throughout the length of the Walk.

Although these and other introductions from many parts of the world form such a striking aspect of the Walk and partly reflect the cosmopolitan nature of Haringey itself, the Walk also supports a wide range of our own wild flowers. A small colony of Common Spotted Orchids persists rather precariously, just a stone's throw from the old trackside, though their few flowers are usually picked each year. This is a rare plant in London, but most of the native plants present are common and widespread. Members of the Pea family are well represented, including seven kinds of Clover and the charming Birds-foot Trefoil. They, and other specialised plants, are particularly well-adapted to grow on the rather poor soils which characterised the old track bed itself, but are intolerant of competition from other more vigorous plants. Today, as a result of the ever increasing dog population, the soils have become "enriched" and several of these plants have declined. Hare's-foot Clover was last seen in 1986 and the Lesser Toadflax is now confined to a few placed on the pathsides of the Parkland Walk Extension. Thus, the flora is never static. Plants come and go as a result of subtle changes to the habitat from year to year.

The great variety of plant-life provides homes for a wide range of animals. Butterflies are probably the best known of the many groups of invertebrate to be seen. Twenty-one species have been recorded, and the Walk is much enlivened by their colourful presence during the summer months. The adult insects are dependent on flowers providing nectar and many species are strongly attracted to Buddleia, which is sometimes named the Butterfly bush. Their caterpillars are often very choosy about the plants they will eat and are unable to survive if the correct food plant is absent. The Common Blue butterfly, sadly no longer common in Haringey, lays its eggs on Bird's-foot Trefoil, which grows along the old trackside and provides food for the caterpillars.

More than sixty species of bird have been recorded along the Walk and about half of these are thought to nest there. A number of them are woodland species and now include for example, all three types of British woodpecker. The Green Woodpecker has been a rather recent arrival, having "discovered" the grassy embankments between Lancaster Road and Florence Road where numerous ant colonies are an irresistable attraction (at least for the woodpeckers!). Tawny Owls are regularly heard, and occasionally seen, in the wooded cutting near Crouch Hill. The density of birds in Spring is well above the national average for this type of habitat and the wooded section between Crouch End Hill and Stanhope Road supports more than four times the average.

Hedgehogs benefit from the proximity of adjacent houses with sympathetic owners. Foxes are tolerated and welcomed in a way that many country people would find hard to believe. Perhaps the most unusual mammal is the Chinese Muntjac, an alsatian-sized deer occasionally seen on the more secluded parts of the Walk. This is a very shy animal, thought to be extending its range into London from breeding populations in Southern Hertfordshire.

A colony of Slow-worms thrives along one grassy embankment. These inconspicuous reptiles are becoming increasingly uncommon in the London area. The colony has been "adopted" by the Haringey branch of the London Wildlife Trust who have been helping to manage the site.

The Parkland Walk is far more, however, than a collection of wild plants and animals, though as we have seen, it supports a remarkable range. It offers above all else, a chance for city people to experience and enjoy wild nature in the heart of London.

Bibliography

Davies, Hunter   *A Walk Along the Tracks* (Hamlyn, 1982,) Chapter 10.
Gilbert, R.   *The Green London Way* (Lawrence and Wishart, 1991),
                                                                    Chapter 11.
Goode, D.   *Wild in London* (Michael Joseph, 1986).

Acknowledgements

David Bevan wishes to thank Dr David Corcoran for helpful discussions, and access to word-processing facilities.

*Mount View Road Bridge, with an abundance of flora
in Londons longest Nature Reserve.*

Notes